Open the Door

A Gathering of Poems and

Among the Books by Elizabeth Yates

Spanning Time: A Diary Keeper Becomes a Writer

Children of the Bible

Amos Fortune, Free Man

Prudence Crandall, Woman of Courage

The Next Fine Day

Someday You'll Write

Is There a Doctor in the Barn?

The Lighted Heart

With Pipe, Paddle and Song:
A Story of French-Canadian Voyageurs

The Road Through Sandwich Notch

Sound Friendships: The Story of Hearing Ear Dogs

A Book of Hours

Pixie Folklore and Legends

The Journeyman

Hue and Cry

OPEN THE DOOR

A Gathering of Poems and Prose Pieces

by

Elizabeth Yates

New Hampshire Antiquarian Society
300 Main Street
Hopkinton, New Hampshire 03229

Copyeditor: Jean Scribner
Proofreader: Barbara Jatkola
Design: The Winzeler Group, M. Kelly May, designer
Photographs: Cover Photograph: Edward M. Crabtree. Back cover photograph: Jane Shaw Jacobs. Text photographs: Nora Unwin (13, 25, 33, 41); New Hampshire Antiquarian Society glass negatives.
Printer: Capital City Press, Inc.

Printed in the United States of America
First edition, 1999

ISBN 1-893894-00-2

Library of Congress Cataloging-in-Publication Data

Yates, Elizabeth, 1905–
Open the door : a gathering of poems and prose pieces / by Elizabeth Yates.
p. cm.
ISBN 1-893894-00-2
1. Country life--New Hampshire Literary collections. 2. New Hampshire--Natural history--Literary collections. 3. Nature Literary collections. I. Title.
PS3547.A745066 1999
818'.5209--dc21 99-22382
CIP

Some of the poems in this volume previously appeared in other works.

"The Crab Tree by the Gate"
From *Spanning Time: A Diary Keeper Becomes a Writer* by Elizabeth Yates, © 1996, Cobblestone Publishing Company, 30 Grove Street, Suite C, Peterborough, NH 03458. Reprinted by permission of the publisher.

"The Holly Speaks"
Copyright (1930s) The Christian Science Publishing Society. Reproduced with permission. All Rights Reserved.

"Early in My Garden"
From *Ribit, The Voice of the Toad,* The Toadstool Bookshops of Keene, Milford & Peterborough, NH, Spring 1998.

Contents

The Poems

S P R I N G

S U M M E R

A U T U M N

W I N T E R

The Prose Pieces

Elizabeth Yates's writing is rich with her observations of the natural world. It is a world from which she takes inspiration and which she has done much to protect.

When Sandwich Notch in the White Mountains was threatened with development in the seventies, Elizabeth gave up a long-awaited adventure in the West to walk the Notch.

A book, *The Road Through Sandwich Notch,* followed, inspiring others to crusade to save the place. As a result, 4,750 acres are now permanently protected as part of the White Mountain National Forest. The campaign is now history, but Elizabeth Yates's legacy in her writing lives on, inspiring people to visit and connect with the Notch.

For her, protecting land preserves history, both natural and human. As a writer, an activist, a donor of land, and a former trustee of the Society for the Protection of New Hampshire Forests, she has, indeed, opened many a door to preserving the natural world that sustains and inspires us.

Jane A. Difley
President/Forester
Society for the Protection of New Hampshire Forests

A poem is about many things. There's some arithmetic in how the words come, the lines break. There's the roll of language spoken. There's continuance of the craft that poets have been practicing a long, long time. But a poem is, especially, about seeing.

Elizabeth sees.

In ancient Egypt it was understood that "the seeing of the eyes, the hearing of the ears, and the breathing of the nose bring messages to the heart." Knowing occurs in the heart, but it is "the tongue which announces what the heart thinks."

Elizabeth sees with her heart. Then she brings us to see what she sees, to know what she's been given to know, "announced" in these collected poems. What has given her meaning in familiar things gives us meaning, too. And we thank her for restoring us to it.

Familiar, simple. Seemingly. Read closely. The "seeing of the eyes, the hearing of the ears, and the breathing of the nose" charge Elizabeth's work with deeper mystery.

My favorite line is "fragrance had a word to say."

You'll find yours.

Mary Lyn Ray

The Poems

SPRING

Two writers, Elizabeth Yates (left) and Elizabeth Gray Vining, talk at Shieling Forest in New Hampshire.

Conversation

There were four people in the room,
one had come with a plant in bloom.

Talk ranged and ideas made their way
while fragrance had a word to say.

The Crab Tree by the Gate

The house had just been built
the year I first bore fruit—
apples with which a child played
in thin September shade.
Cold strengthened me and when
spring came round again
white blossoms crowned my head.
"Look!" the little girl cried.
"Our tiny crab tree is a bride!"

When she wore bridal dress
I had attained my height.
A branch of mine could rest
on the wall to the west;
another reached to salute
the east with ripening fruit.
Baskets of apples I bore,
plenty rode my golden tide,
but with every spring I was a bride.

Families changed in the house
and my apples were used
for jelly and wine, sliced,
put into jars and spiced.
A nest rode me like an ark.
Woodpeckers drilled my bark.
Years were so many leaves
tossed windward and wide,
but with every spring I was a bride.

Storms swept over my limbs,
ice bent my branches down,
but only the weight of my gold
ever broke a bough's hold.
Gnarled now and deep of root,
robust bearer of fruit,
I give shade, yield to wind,
stand breasting life's tide,
for with every spring I am a bride.

From My Window

A vixen loped across the field,
such grace I saw revealed.

A doe stood in a patch of shade
and gazed around her unafraid.

A squirrel darted up a tree,
chuckling in hilarity.

And I, awash with gratitude,
knew the bliss of solitude.

Planting Peas at Twilight

There had been rain and sun
and the earth lay mellow,
seeds were set from a hand,
each one an orb, each yellow
with tendrils ready to uncoil
when havened by the warmth of soil.
The moon that night looked down on rows
of seeds, their promise in repose.

The Deer Come Out of the Woods

Did you hear them whistling,
whistling in the orchard?
Blossoms white above them,
white against the night?
Did you see hooves flashing,
flashing on the grass,
grass ashine with silver,
dewy wet and white?

Did you see them coming,
coming from the pine woods,
stepping high and proudly
through the flowing brook?
Did you see them frolic,
frolic in the orchard,
at the darkest hour
when only stars could look?

Joyful as the blossoms,
blossoms white above them,
joyful as the dewdrops
star-tipping the grass;
did you hear them whistling,
whistling to each other,
gay and glad as springtime,
fleet as winds that pass?

The Tree Speaks for Itself

Seeded by wind or bird and demurely
growing mid vegetables,

I gained a height where I had to reach
out and speak for myself:

So I was moved, my roots were severed
to search for new sustenance.

It was a shock, but the hands that
did it were tender

And under their touch I felt myself
reaching into new soil.

Now I salute the sun in its rising and
at night I challenge the stars.

Marvel at the Moment

Today I have been on Olympus,
cloud shrouded, serene,
or was it Sinai,
that fire-shattered demesne?
Or was it Eden,
that place so eminent?
Exactness is irrelevant.
God's finger touching mine
made creation intimate, immediate,
divine.

To a Song Sparrow Nesting Outside My Window

I have a little house,
its roof is snug and tight,
its windows frame wide views
of mutable delight.

Your house is roofed with sky
and sheltered by a tree,
I work with words
and you in minstrelsy.

With gifts we grace
the world we share,
making of songs
a way of prayer.

Requiem

I shall not see your face again
nor hold your hand in mine;
but kindness has a broader reach
and joy I can define.

No letters now, no dear trysts kept,
we meet without design,
the essential you, compound of love,
released from boundary and time.

Visitation

Spring is at the door
Oh, not the door to my garden,
that will come later,
but the door that opens to my house.
In one hand she held parsnips,
released from their winter hold,
in the other she held mayflowers!

What matters the weather
when riches come together?
Parsnips and mayflowers,
bounty at all hours!

SUMMER

Elizabeth tends to her border of nasturtiums at Shieling.

Mountain Blueberry

Obscurely growing, in land so poor that
    nothing else will thrive
save spindle spires of hardhack,
and stubborn roots of sumac
with low-lying juniper;
familiar of loneliness
and of the wind's caress,
a wealth of blue fruit weighs the
    gnarled stems down
and each blueberry wears a tiny crown.

These once were pastures, but the waste-
    land now is host to bushes
blue as dawn's first thrust, and high,
intimate of far-flung sky
and the wild woodland robin.
Here heaven's benevolence
links with earth's affluence,
and none are present who require renown—
yet each small berry wears a tiny crown.

Random the Garden

I've flowers in my garden!
"But you haven't a garden."
Oh yes. It's a big field:
There's yarrow and clover now,
And in a little while daisies
and mustard and Queen Anne's lace.
They come, one by one,
and the sun and the rain are
the gardeners.

Sea Favor

It should be a diamond
or an aquamarine;
it could be an opal
with a translucent sheen.

Candid as a moonbeam,
smooth as the sand,
firm as the adamant,
shaped for the hand.

Not really precious,
yet that isn't true,
for it's a medium
to bring my love to you.

And you will understand,
seeing the beauty more
in the smooth seashell
found on a sandy shore.

Climbing

Long and free-swinging, the stride adapts
to the path's upward tilt;
feet know the spring of turf,
the frequent stubbing at rocks,
the chance slip, while hands grasp securely
the smooth bark of a beech,
the fissured bark of a maple.
Slower the pace becomes,
the breath more deeply drawn
as the path narrows, steepens,
and feet move to find firmness.
Leap now as hands make sure the step
by grasping rough warmth of granite.
Quicken the push though the heart pounds
And breath is short, then stand
wind-circled and face the nothing higher.
Across the valley hills have been rising
and the gaze no longer reaches,
but rests on other heights.

Come Saturday

He likes to fish in hidden pools
and she in open water,
but he's at work all week and she's
alone. Lake fishing from a boat
is what they'll do together,
lengthening a line, bobbing a float.

There are cool depths within the mind
a weekend gives them time to savor:
no stock may nibble at their hooks
for talking has the richest flavor.

He likes to fish in hidden pools
and she in open water.

On Seeing Black-eyed Susans in a Field

The flowers look up into the skies
with wide brown wondering eyes.

Grasses wave,
roots grow deep,
winds brush low,
insects creep,
cicadas call
summer's song,
days draw out
warm and long.

Birds wheeling in low flight
see the field to their delight.

AUTUMN

Elizabeth and Fame.

Rain in October

Have you seen trees
glittering with golden leaves,
the sun's illumination
giving widespread radiation?
Then this is beauty:
a world gay decked and vivid hued,
limpid air, cerulean skies
and everything with light imbued.

But on a day
of rain and skies low hung and gray,
have you seen variegated leaves
shining though the weather grieves?
Then this is wonder:
a somber world with light so thin
that it is tenuous, yet burning
as if the glory were within.

Au Revoir

I thought I could not bear to see
        the zinnias go—
color of fire they were against the
        garden's green:
brick red and crimson, scarlet, gold
        and flame,
fawn and maroon, cerise and coralline.

        Frost came one night,
        finis in its track:
        flowers turned to cinders,
        foliage went black.

There were no zinnias left to crown
        the garden's year,
but on the lofty maple towering overhead
leaves were burning skyward, wind-driven flames,
copper and saffron, cinnabar and red.

Thanksgiving

One day is all too short
to hold the blessings of a year,
yet how much richer the year
for this one day.
From its height I scan
the peaks of joy, achievement, bliss,
service and comradeship.
Forgotten are the valleys between,
yet had they not been
no height had followed after.

What is this light suffusing all I see,
this warmth embracing all I know?
These are my thanks and in them
is my wealth.

Musing

The fire was not lit for warmth
but company,
tongues of flame talk vividly
to me.
When conversation ends,
the embers glowing red
admit with satisfaction
that enough's been said.

Query

What is this stillness that we feel,
this quiet avowal of things that be?
What does it mean, what presage,
is it the mellowing that some call age?

Rx

He said it softly:
I heard it in my inner ear,
"You may always need a hand to hold,
or a staff to bear your weight."
I know that Hand. It is not far,
it never will be far.

WINTER

Elizabeth and Fame brave the New Hampshire snow.

The Holly Speaks

O Holly—your berries red
are so high above my head!
Out of my reach, yes quite,
and so temptingly bright!
Jewels set in wintry skies,
but only for my eyes.
O Holly—have you no words?

"Yes, I must remember my birds."

O Holly—your leaves prick
my fingers when I pick
even one branch, but if I
could only reach up high
I'd have berries, boughs and all.
Not a prickle however small
is on those branches, but leaves
smooth-turned in glistening sheaves.
O Holly—have you no words?

"Yes, I must remember my birds."

Those hard fruits the birds will shun
they'll not have them, no, not one!

"No, not now while there's food,
but should the winter brood
and the earth freeze to stone
and the hips be all gone,
the birds will flock around
that which hardness has kept sound."

Bitter as wind from the east,
can the birds call that a feast?

"Feasts are made of answered needs,
forgetting for what it pleads
a bird is happy to dine
on such berries as mine
from a table of green
by the wind swept clean.
What matter bitter with sweet to follow,
spring on the wing of a swallow?
Spring at the forest's foot,
a-stir in each primrose root?"

O Holly—I love your words!

"Yes, I must remember my birds."

Between House and Road

There was a tree that reached up to the sky
and gripped the earth with searching roots,
more than a hundred years it had stood
serving in the ways a tree can serve.
But time was taking its toll;
limbs could no longer bear without breaking
under great weights of snow,
nor could branches yield to the wind's sweep.
Near a house and a busy road,
the tree had become a hazard. It had to go.
"You must miss it," people said to the one who lived near.
She answered "Yes," and she answered "No."
"Yes, because it was beautiful and gave shade."
"No, because it lives on in memory
and is sheltered in my heart."

Farm Wife

She used to bake bread every Tuesday,
half a dozen loaves and a pie or two,
then a scrap of dough left over would do
for a tin of biscuits. Eliza May
(that was her name) baked one morning, a sight
of her good things crowded the pantry shelves;
then she took sick. We cooked dinner ourselves.
The doctor came, but Liza died that night.
There wasn't much to do but bury her
and it was hard for us to break the ground,
for snow lay heavy and the wind was bleak.
In winter you can't get a minister
so I read the words. But Liza stayed round
awhile, for we were at her bread all week.

Conviction

You do not need to raise your voice.
I shall not argue with you
nor do I need to be convinced.
I am convinced
that violence of any kind
is wrong.

Carpe Diem

Five poems wrote themselves
across my world today,
fragments of errant Beauty,
hastening on their way:

a race of clouds bright
with dawn's intensity of light;
a landward gull upheld
in circles wind-impelled;
leaves whose tattered vesture
mocked the wind's romantic gesture;
a saffron sunset barred by black
fast upon night's scurrying track;
and bare slim branches brushing high
against a leaden wintry sky.

Five poems wrote themselves
with wind on air today,
lovely though perishable,
in words to stay.

The Cyclamen and the Wind

Beyond
was a flawless expanse of snow
from which slim trees rose dark and nude.
The wind swept high, the wind swung low,
ecstatic in its solitude.
Scattering drifts in rampaging delight,
the wind roared on in the path of the night.

Within
was a cyclamen full and white,
flowers poised like birds to wing a world,
buoyantly resting, gay and light.
The pot was only where roots lay curled
for the cyclamen was free. And the wind,
was it more so, being undisciplined?

Before Dawn in Bethlehem

A cat came by
hearing a cry.

To the crib from the ground
she leapt to see whence the sound;
then settling herself she purred,
but only the small one heard.

That lullaby
silenced the cry.

A Shepherd Speaks for His Dog

The sheep were safely folded
and with so much light in the sky
I saw no need to stay with them;
no skulking jackal or lurking wolf
would be abroad when night was like day.
So he came with me, staying close,
almost foot to foot, it was his way,
and when we reached the manger
it was the babe's feet he put his nose to.
Happy he was and his tail moved so much
it stirred a breeze near the child's head,
cooling the air and changing it.
The baby smiled, and hand reached to stroke fur.
Then we went back to the flock.

There Was a Dog

So many people, the old dog thought,
but I'll keep close to my master.

He followed him up to a wooden trough
and what he saw made his tail wag faster,
for the wide-eyed child had the shepherd look;
it was something the dog had never mistook.

They didn't stay, work was back on the hill
but the old dog's tail couldn't keep still;
it was not the wind or the pace of their going
but something the old dog couldn't help knowing.

Then a familiar hand was placed on his head
as they walked along fast and faster,
"Friend," a familiar voice softly said,
"I think I have found my Master."

A Cornish Legend

Nobody saw the spider
who scurried across the floor;
long after the shepherds had left,
she had come to adore.

Mary, wearied by travel
and worn from birthing a child,
leaned toward her Joseph,
touched his lips and smiled.

"Let us sleep," she said to him,
"the visitors all have gone,
and night is a sheltering arm
that will hold us until dawn."

Creeping into the manger
the spider spun a web,
making a gossamer cover
across the infant's bed.

To and fro she crissed and crossed
with her filament line,
out of herself she gave her gift
of delicate design.

When soldiers searched the stable
to allay a mad king's fears,
they saw two weary strangers
sleeping free from cares.

They scoffed at Herod's orders
as they reported the sight,
"Nothing but dust and cobwebs
and only a star for a light."

So the child slept secure
while the hours moved on,
and the spider disappeared
when her work was done.

Mary was first to awaken
and, brushing the web away,
folded the child in her bosom.
"Joseph," she said, "it's day."

Post Christmas

Do not try to hold it overlong,
this day that is the glory of the year.

Love it. Live in it while it lasts,
delight in all its gaiety and cheer.

Then let it pass with other days
into the pattern of the year's full chart,

only, as another in distant time,
keep fast its wonder to ponder in the heart.

The Prose Pieces

Early in My Garden

The short days of winter have been yielding as light has come with lengthening days. The earth is released from its covering of snow and ice, but it is still sodden. My garden draws me and rewards me when I discover a few tiny knobs just breaking through, barely visible. Coming back the next day they are more evident: the first, the very first, "Adonis." Day after day I watch them, bending down to touch them. Soon they reveal their tightly folded petals with a hint of color. The firmness of the ground gives to their insistence. The hint of color shows in a surround of leaves that have more of an earthy brown to them than green. Day after day I watch them, talk to them, cheer them on, or perhaps it is they that cheer me on when the wind blows cold and snow flurries mask the near world. A few inches they have come and I can count six flowers-to-be; last year there were only three. They are tightly closed but their determination matches my own as winter's retreat becomes spring's renewing touch. Now they are taller than my hand and still growing. Now they are opening, showing their true color, and the leaves are reaching out, lacey and deep green. Three weeks it has been and on the third they open fully—little golden chalices offering their light to the sun that has been summoning them. Seeing them now they are no longer hints but promises of the medley of bloom that is the garden's way. My heart, like Wordsworth's, "with pleasure fills and dances with the daffodils."

Midsummer Meeting

I saw them as I was crossing the field, so I hastened my step to sit beside them. They were growing against the stone wall, and some had almost reached the height of the wall, others were just above the tangled grass. They were blue as I knew they would be, a soft slate blue and tightly closed.

"Bottle gentians," I said in greeting, and then, dropping down beside them, I asked the question, "What is the secret that you will not tell?"

Their silence, their stature, their calm repose rebuked me. What dignity they had! Their petals, folded tightly inward, would not open and reveal themselves in fragrance as most flowers did, and I admired them for standing their ground as they did. But at season's end the flowers would turn brown and dry, then split slightly, and seeds for another growing would find their way into the earth. Fingering one of the gentians, my touch traveled down the petal to the stem, and there I spied the tiny white patch that indicated an opening for a bee. Feelers could force an entrance in their search for honey but not fingers. In their way the gentians were saying something to me, and I replied, withdrawing my question.

"I will not ask, for I have a secret too and so share wonder with you."

Walking hiveward across the field, the treasure I carried had no weight.

Time for Myself

There were things I could do, should do, but there was nothing that I had to do, so I took time for myself and went to my garden. Alone. The sun will be my keeper, and when shade from a tall tree falls aslant me, it will tell me it is time to leave. A book is on my lap, but I doubt that it will be opened. So much is happening in this small space for me to attend to and heed. There is stillness and activity. A bird, hopping near, looks at me, aware of my presence and fully acceptant of it. A bee is seeking honey from a flower whose petals are wide open. A frog bounces by. All and more of their kind come into the stillness, seeking what they need as I am, and our needs though different are being fulfilled. Time does not matter for any of us. We are deep in peace.

Looking down at some earth that I had smoothed over newly planted seeds a few days ago, I can discern a tiny breaking in the soil. Already the seeds are at work. I feel their energy. In another few days, blest by sun and rain and the long quiet of night, they will reach up and out. Green shoots will appear above the soil like little hands clapping at their release from the dark.

Did I think I was alone? The definition is "All plus one." I take delight in one small word that has a wondrous reach.

Now the shade has found me, telling me it is time to return to the house. I shall, not reluctantly, for I am filled with a deep quiet and the garden is in me.

Something Overheard

The moment was brief, but it has lived in my memory. Someone in a gathering of writers was proclaiming for moral strength in poetry, and Robert P.T. Coffin, the long-loved voice of Maine, was shaking his head. "I wouldn't think about that too much," he said. "The poet has to get his meaning through in a way other than the preacher—by making something indelible, by quickening appreciation. Don't use things bigger than your comprehension. Choose simple things to illustrate the whole, things that are yours, not windy abstractions. Philosophy is death to poetry, it will clip an angel's wings. Take the Bible, it's the most concrete book ever written, the most beautiful; poetry yes, but simple everyday facts. Jesus talked about father-son relationships, neighbors, bread, flowers of the field; tangible things that people understood." He paused, then spoke with new emphasis, "It's what MacLeish said, 'A poem should not mean but be.'" There may have been more, but that is what I remember and wanted to hold on to. And holding, my mind went back to something Beatrix Potter had once written, that when she felt her style needed chastening she read the King James version of the Bible.

These writings reflect some of the simple things that speak to me and that have given me meaning through the years—trees and creatures, country ways, hills into mountains, and quiet.

About the Author

Elizabeth Yates's books, side by side, fill seven-plus feet of bookshelf in her home. She calls the books her family. They are as varied as New Hampshire weather and span five productive decades. With this new collection of poetry, the family grows.

Her books—thin and thick, tall and small—attest to her longevity as a writer and the exceptional range of her work. She writes for children and adults; poetry, fiction, and nonfiction. Some of her stories are historical. Some contemporary. Some light, playful; others serious, philosophical. Some, like the award-winning *Amos Fortune, Free Man,* seem timeless.

Amos Fortune won the Newbery Medal in 1951. In 1999 it remains a popular choice for sixth-grade and other reading lists nationwide. The book's appeal grows stronger and stronger. Why? Elizabeth's explanation is "I told the story simply." Another explanation might be that she simply told the story with an exquisite command of her craft.

She has spent a lifetime learning, refining, and exploring that craft. She inspires not only with her work but with her approach to it, which she shares generously with those who walk the same road, but are not quite so far along. For many years, she taught at various writers' conferences where new writers "hoping to write and some writing already" came to study with experienced ones. Over time, the words of many of her students found their way into print. Teaching was hard work, she says, but her years with the writers' conferences were among the "most rewarding" of her life, especially worthwhile, she says, because "you get the feeling you can turn them a little."

One gets the feeling she has turned many writers, and that her influence lives on in the accomplishments of more than one generation.

She still reads works-in-progress and meets with aspiring writers in her home, offering advice and encouragement. She continues to share her experiences with children. She recalls one boy in particular who bravely asked, "Has aging improved your writing?"

"Of course, yes," she replied. "All of life from the first moment right up 'til the last is learning."

To find stories and poems and essays, Elizabeth looks inward. Ideas come to her. They grow within her and with her. Some want to be poems or novels for children; others choose memoir. Her contributions to the literature of New Hampshire (and the world) are many. But especially significant is her career's testimonial to the value of trusting yourself and your ideas, then crafting those ideas to fruition.

Her poem "The Tree Speaks for Itself" came to her in a flash of insight. It's about a real tree in her garden: a tree that spoke to her. It needed attention and thrived when it got it. That poem could just as easily be about the ideas Elizabeth Yates nurtures into books, and the many writers she has nurtured and encouraged and inspired over the years.

Rebecca Rule

The New Hampshire Antiquarian Society, founded as The Philomathic Club by three Hopkinton residents in 1859, began as a literary discussion group and was incorporated under its current name in 1875.

The Society provides the greater Hopkinton community with:
exhibits, programs, lectures, tours related to local and state history
projects for children
school tours
special events such as the popular summer art show
a museum shop filled with works of local artisans
publications
a library for historical and genealogical research

11-19-12 $2-@ Toadstool